RP **STUDIO**

PHILADELPHIA

RP Studio™
Hachette Book Group
1290 Avenue of the Americas, New York, NY 10104
www.runningpress.com
@Running_Press

Printed in China

First Edition: September 2020

Published by RP Studio, an imprint of Perseus Books, LLC, a subsidiary of Hachette Book Group, Inc. The RP Studio name and logo is a trademark of the Hachette Book Group.

The publisher is not responsible for websites (or their content) that are not owned by the publisher.

Text by Nathan Schmidt

Design by Celeste Joyce

ISBN: 978-0-7624-7129-4 (hardcover)

1010

10 9 8 7 6 5 4 3 2 1

FLIP ME!

Corgi is a Welsh term that means "dwarf dog."
Small, but mighty.

Corgis are affectionate and loyal dogs, and love being involved in the family pack and all of their activities.

Corgis were originally bred to herd cattle and horses.

Corgis aren't cowards. Think of their size relative to the size of the animals they herd. Right?

The plural of "corgi" may be "corgis" or "corgwn."
But two corgis are always cuter than one.

Corgis can live up to 15 years, with females living longer than males. One wise old corgi, Bluey, lived to be 29!

There are two breeds of corgis: the Pembroke Welsh Corgi and the Cardigan Welsh Corgi. The Pembroke is the more widely recognized corgi with a short or no tail, while the Cardigan is best known for its longer tail and fashionable sweaters.

In Welsh folklore, fairies and elves used corgis to pull fairy coaches, and corgis also worked as herding dogs, herding fairy cattle herds.

Corgis are the favorite dog breed of Queen Elizabeth II. She has owned more than 30! Not all at once.

Queen Elizabeth II's first corgi, Dookie (his formal name was The Duke), was a gift from King George VI in 1933.

Corgis are known to enjoy climbing to higher places to have a better view.

Corgis have been around since at least 1107 CE, when they were brought to the UK from Belgium.

If a corgi was used as a working dog in the UK, it had to have its tail docked. The Pembroke Corgi has since been bred to have a stubby little tail, or no tail at all. Some dogs still have their tails docked, though the corgis would prefer if you didn't.

Corgis shed constantly, but each hair is dropped with love.

Legend has it that fairy warriors would ride the corgi into battle. This is supposedly where the corgi got the saddle-shaped markings on its coat.

Corgis are a very smart breed, and eager to please. Given the right training, they could theoretically do your taxes.

Despite their adorably chubby wittle legs, corgis are very athletic, and compete in many dog agility contests.

Corgis generally weigh up to 30 pounds. Like most dogs, they would like to weigh much, much more, but it's not good for their health.

Long-coated corgis are known as "Fluffies."

While their lineage is not fully known, corgis seem to have descended from Swedish Vallhunds as well as Spitz-type dogs, such as Siberian Huskies, Akita Inus, and Samoyeds.

A corgi "sploot" is when a corgi stretches out on its belly with its back legs stretched out flat behind them. The "sploot" is also accompanied by squeals of delight from any onlookers.

Corgi butts are sometimes mistaken for
two fluffy loaves of bread.

Corgis may be small, but their bark is BIG!

A corgi asleep on its back will look remarkably like a stuffed animal. You may be tempted to pick them up, but keep in mind that they also need their beauty sleep. *Shhhhh.*

The size of the corgi helps with their herding. They're able to nip at the heels of wayward cattle while being small enough to duck under any kicks.

Vikings were big fans of corgis and would bring them along to all their outdoor activities, i.e., looting and pillaging.

Corgis, despite being in the chunky, stubby little leg club, are not closely related to Dachshunds. Apart from being dogs, that is.

Corgis have been known to be heroes, saving people from being injured by falling branches, tracking and finding lost people, and just being an uplifting presence.

Under ancient Welsh law, stealing a corgi would result in a hefty fine. Don't steal dogs.

Date: _____

What do you call a corgi in disguise? In-*corg*-nito.

Queen Elizabeth II was given one of her corgis, Susan, on her eighteenth birthday. Many of her subsequent corgis were descendents of Susan.

Variations of the "sploot," part 1: half sploot—only one back leg extended.

The anime Cowboy Bebop features a corgi named Ein who specializes in computer hacking.

Variations of the corgi "sploot," part 2: side sploot—back legs are both to one side.

Sploots aren't just adorable: they also help corgis stretch out their hips and cool off after vigorous play.

Variations of the corgi "sploot," part 3: upside down or reverse sploot—on back instead of stomach, back legs extended.

Governor Jerry Brown of California named his corgi Sutter Brown, the First Dog of California. He was beloved for his licks across the aisle.

Variations of the corgi "sploot," part 4: pancake sploot—all four legs fully extended out.

Corgis are known for being easy to train and eager to please. However, they are not obsequious; they will judge you.

Corgis can be found wearing a few varieties of coats, such as Sable, Black and Tan, and Red. Corgis may or may not have white markings.

Corgi beach days have been happening in California since 2012. One beach day saw over 1,200 corgis in attendance. The cuteness was historic.

Corgis generally get along with other breeds, but beware! If corgis get into a fight with another dog, they will still be really cute. Nonetheless, break it up.

There is no such thing as a subtle corgi walk.

Corgi ears are very large for the size of their heads and bodies. Their ears will usually stand upright when they are 4 to 6 months old.

Corgis can swim, but their fluffy butts float so much that they spend most of the time trying to keep their heads out of the water.

Why do cowboys get corgis? To get a long little doggie.

Corgi butts should not be used as a floatation device in case of an emergency water landing.

Puppies that are the result of mixing a corgi with any other breed are *scientifically* cuter than the original, non-corgi breed. It's science.

Corgis are fast! Those floofy little legs can move!

In Japan, fluffy corgi butts are known as *momo*, the Japanese word for "peach," due to their resemblance.

Roedd hi'n fore braf o wanwyn ac
roedd y Dewin Doeth yn hapus iawn.
Cododd yn gynnar i gasglu madarch.

1

"Mi wn i pwy fyddai'n hoffi'r madarch yma," meddai. "Af at Ceridwen a gofyn iddi gael brecwast gyda fi. Mmmm, madarch."

Casglodd y madarch bach gwyn
a'u rhoi mewn basged.
Casglodd lond basged.

Roedd yn mwmian canu wrth gerdded.
"Rwyt ti'n hapus iawn heddiw,"
meddai ceiliog y rhedyn.

"Mae'n fore braf o wanwyn ac mae gen i
lond basged o fadarch,"
meddai'r Dewin Doeth.
"Rydw i'n mynd i'w bwyta i frecwast."

"Hoffet ti glywed cyfrinach?"
gofynnodd y Dewin Doeth.
"Hoffwn," atebodd ceiliog y rhedyn.

"Rydw i mewn cariad!"
meddai'r Dewin Doeth.

"Dyna hyfryd ar fore braf o wanwyn,"
meddai ceiliog y rhedyn.
"Rheswm da dros ganu."
Llamodd ceiliog y rhedyn i ffwrdd yn sionc.

Cribodd y Dewin Doeth ei wallt
a sythodd ei het.
Curodd ar ddrws ogof Tu Hwnt.
Cnoc, cnoc, cnoc.
Pesychodd…

"Bore da, Ceridwen!"
meddai'r Dewin Doeth.
"Dim ond anrheg fach i'r wrach orau
yn y byd!"

"Bobol bach, Dewin Doeth, chi sydd yna!"
meddai Ceridwen yn syn.
"Rydych chi wedi galw'n gynnar braidd."

"A dweud y gwir, dydw i ddim wedi cael
fy mrecwast eto," meddai Ceridwen.
"Yn hollol," meddai'r Dewin Doeth.
"Dyna pam rydw i wedi galw."

"Edrychwch!" meddai gan ddal y fasged
o flaen ei thrwyn hir.
"Llond basged o fadarch ffres. Meddwl
roeddwn i y byddech yn hoffi madarch
i frecwast."

"Tyrchod o'r gwrychoedd!
Na fyddwn wir!" atebodd Ceridwen.
"Mae'n gas gen i fadarch.
Maen nhw'n fy ngwneud i'n sâl!"

"O, Rwdins Rachub!" meddai'r Dewin Doeth.
"Rydw i wedi difetha popeth – a minnau'n
meddwl ei fod yn syniad campus."

"Peidiwch â phoeni," meddai Ceridwen.
"Cewch frecwast yr un fath. Mae gen i
baned boeth a llyfr bach meddal i chi...
Beth sy'n bod, Dewin Doeth?"

"Mae'n gas gen i lyfrau, Ceridwen.
Maen nhw'n fy ngwneud i'n sâl.
Dydw i ddim yn hoffi darllen llyfrau
na'u bwyta. O diar mi."

Cafodd Ceridwen syniad campus.
"Bwytwch chi'r madarch, Dewin Doeth,
ac mi wna innau fwyta'r llyfrau."

"Siort orau," meddai'r Dewin Doeth.
Roedd y ddau yn hapus iawn yn rhannu'r
bwrdd brecwast gyda'i gilydd.

19

Ond dyna'r tro olaf i'r Dewin Doeth
gynnig madarch i Ceridwen!